COUNTRIES OF THE WORLD

THE CARIBBEAN

John Griffiths

With photographs by John Griffiths
and John Wright

Illustrated by Malcolm Walker

The Bookwright Press
New York · 1989

Titles in this series

Australia	Italy
Canada	Japan
The Caribbean	The Netherlands
China	New Zealand
France	Pakistan
Great Britain	Spain
Greece	The United States
India	West Germany

Cover *The port of Pointe-a-Pitre in Guadeloupe, part of the French Caribbean.*

Opposite *Gibbs Beach on Barbados, one of the many islands that make up the Caribbean region.*

© Copyright 1989 Wayland (Publishers) Ltd

First published in the United States by
The Bookwright Press
387 Park Avenue South
New York NY 10016

First published in 1989 by
Wayland (Publishers) Ltd
61 Western Road, Hove
East Sussex BN3 1JD, England

Library of Congress Cataloging-in-Publication Data
Griffiths, John. 1942 Apr. 5–
   The Caribbean/by John Griffiths.
     p. cm. — (Countries of the world)
Bibliography: p.
Includes index.
Summary: Introduces the geography, history, culture, and economy of the Caribbean.
   ISBN 0–531–18274–6
   1. Caribbean Area – Juvenile literature   [1. Caribbean Area.]   I. Title.   II. Series: Countries of the world (New York, N.Y.)
F2161.5.G75 1989
972.9–dc19   88–28782
                                                    CIP
Printed in Italy by G. Canale and C.S.p.A., Turin   AC

Contents

All words that appear in **bold** in the text are explained in the glossary on page 46.

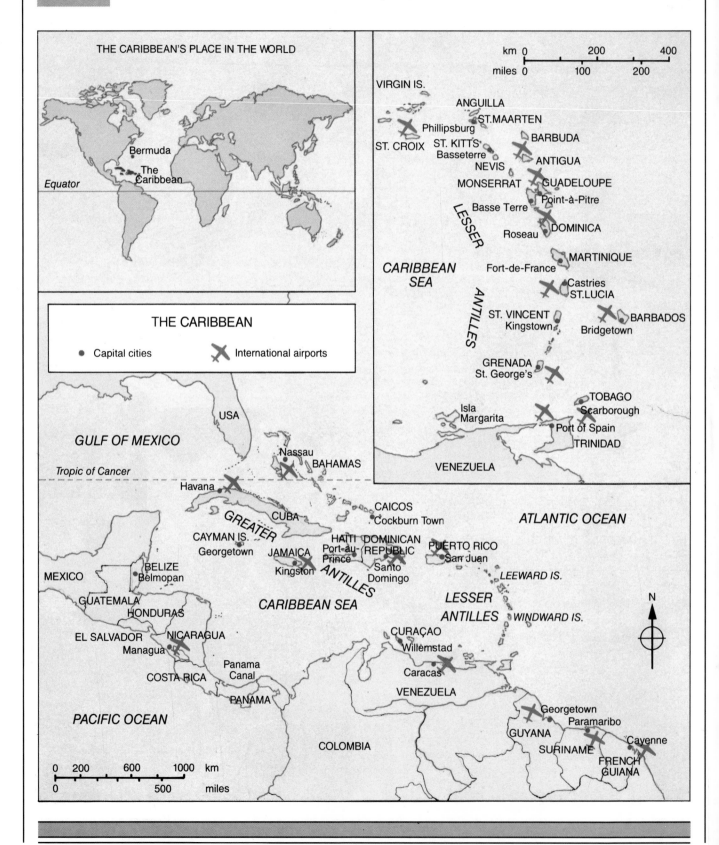

1

THE CARIBBEAN'S PLACE IN THE WORLD

Bermuda

The Caribbean

Equator

THE CARIBBEAN

- Capital cities
- ✈ International airports

km 0 — 200 — 400
miles 0 — 100 — 200

VIRGIN IS.

ANGUILLA

ST.MAARTEN

Phillipsburg

ST. CROIX

ST. KITTS
Basseterre

NEVIS

BARBUDA

ANTIGUA

MONSERRAT

GUADELOUPE

Basse Terre

Point-à-Pitre

Roseau

DOMINICA

LESSER

CARIBBEAN
SEA

MARTINIQUE

Fort-de-France

Castries
ST.LUCIA

ANTILLES

ST. VINCENT
Kingstown

BARBADOS
Bridgetown

GRENADA
St. George's

Isla
Margarita

TOBAGO
Scarborough

Port of Spain
TRINIDAD

VENEZUELA

GULF OF MEXICO

USA

Tropic of Cancer

Havana

Nassau

BAHAMAS

CAICOS
Cockburn Town

ATLANTIC OCEAN

GREATER

CUBA

CAYMAN IS.
Georgetown

JAMAICA
Kingston

HAITI
Port-au-Prince

DOMINICAN
REPUBLIC

Santo
Domingo

PUERTO RICO
San Juan

LEEWARD IS.

ANTILLES

MEXICO

BELIZE
Belmopan

CARIBBEAN SEA

LESSER
ANTILLES

WINDWARD IS.

GUATEMALA

HONDURAS

EL SALVADOR

NICARAGUA
Managua

CURAÇAO
Willemstad

Caracas

N

COSTA RICA

Panama
Canal

VENEZUELA

PANAMA

PACIFIC OCEAN

COLOMBIA

Georgetown
Paramaribo

GUYANA

Cayenne

SURINAME

FRENCH
GUIANA

0 — 200 — 600 — 1000 km
0 — 500 — miles

When you think about the Caribbean, which countries come to your mind? Ideas about exactly which countries belong to the region are constantly changing. For many people, the Caribbean used to consist of the West Indies, the string of islands curving from Cuba southward to Trinidad. But that is only part of the picture.

If you look at the map, you will see that the United States and some countries of Central America extend into the Caribbean Sea. However, the United States and Mexico are not thought of as part of the Caribbean, although they have played an important role in the region. Other countries that lie outside the Caribbean Sea, for example Bermuda and the Bahamas (which are in the Atlantic Ocean), are thought of as part of the Caribbean, because of their climate and culture.

Two Central American countries that belong to the Caribbean are Belize and Nicaragua. In the past Belize (once called British Honduras) was closely linked with the West Indies.

Nicaragua also has close links with the Caribbean. The people who live on the Caribbean coast of Nicaragua are mainly of African origin, like many of the people who live on the islands of the Caribbean. They were brought to Nicaragua by the British as slaves and speak English, rather than Spanish. In this way they have more in common with Caribbean people than other Nicaraguans and Central Americans.

Farther away, on the northeastern coast of South America, the countries Guyana, French Guiana and Suriname all belong to the Caribbean. Venezuela is another South American country that is becoming increasingly linked with other Caribbean countries.

Although this is rather complicated, it shows that countries belong to the Caribbean for many reasons. Their geographical location is often not so important as their **culture** and the people who settled there in the past.

This view of the port of St. Georges in Grenada shows the mixed architecture and tropical vegetation, that are typical of the Caribbean.

2 Land and climate

There are thousands of islands that make up the Caribbean. Cuba is the largest at 70,000 sq km (43,500 sq mi). Hispaniola (Haiti and the Dominican Republic) is the next largest at 43,000 sq km (26,700 sq mi). Many islands, like Grenada, Dominica, Guadeloupe, Montserrat, northern Hispaniola, southeastern Cuba, and eastern Jamaica are ruggedly mountainous, steep and unsuitable for settlement. Barbados and Antigua, on the other hand, are flat. The center and west of Cuba consists of gently sloping mountains set in richly **fertile** plains.

The large northern islands, Cuba, Hispaniola, Jamaica and Puerto Rico, are known as the Greater Antilles.

The town of St. Pierre in Martinique nestles at the foot of Mount Pelée. This volcano erupted in 1902, killing 30,000 people.

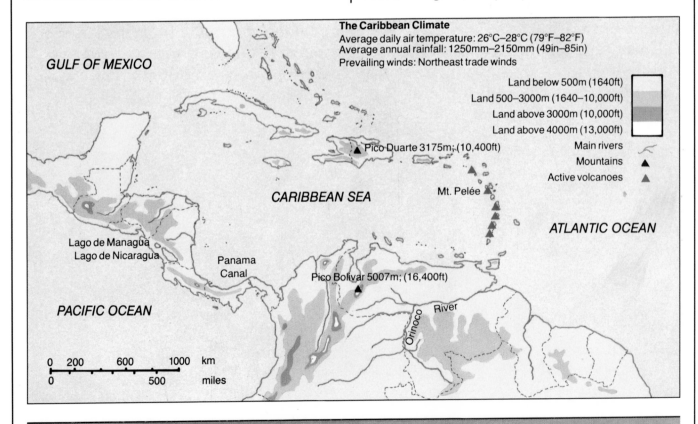

The Caribbean Climate
Average daily air temperature: 26°C–28°C (79°F–82°F)
Average annual rainfall: 1250mm–2150mm (49in–85in)
Prevailing winds: Northeast trade winds

Land below 500m (1640ft)
Land 500–3000m (1640–10,000ft)
Land above 3000m (10,000ft)
Land above 4000m (13,000ft)

Main rivers
Mountains
Active volcanoes

GULF OF MEXICO

Pico Duarte 3175m; (10,400ft)

CARIBBEAN SEA

Mt. Pelée

ATLANTIC OCEAN

Lago de Managua
Lago de Nicaragua

Panama Canal

Pico Bolivar 5007m; (16,400ft)

PACIFIC OCEAN

Orinoco River

0   200   600   1000   km
0   500   miles

Left The island of Aruba, part of the Dutch Antilles, is rocky and like a desert in places.

Below The tropical climate of the Caribbean allows beautiful plants, like the white frangipani, to flourish.

The southern, smaller islands form the Lesser Antilles.

All three Caribbean countries in South America – Guyana, Suriname and French Guiana – are huge and, as yet, barely **exploited**. Guyana, for example, possesses vast agricultural land and is rich in minerals.

All the Caribbean islands enjoy a magnificent climate that favors the tropical agriculture of the region as well as tourism. The rainy season lasts from May to November. The warm winter season is mainly dry apart from occasional showers of rain. The disadvantage of the Caribbean climate is the hurricane season, which can occur at any time in the summer and autumn. A whole city, Belize, was destroyed in just one such hurricane in 1931. In 1988 the region was struck by Hurricane Gilbert, the worst this century. Hurricanes have caused chaos for Caribbean agricultural products, like bananas and coffee, on numerous occasions. Weather forecasting and satellite observations can predict the course of hurricanes more accurately, but their devastating power is still felt.

3 A wealth of wildlife

After Columbus had landed on Cuba on Sunday, October 28, 1492, he wrote in his diary that he had set foot on "the most beautiful isle that eyes have ever seen." In a letter to the King and Queen of Spain, after whom he first named Cuba, he described it further:

The remaining rainforests of the Caribbean are very rich in trees, flowers and animals. This photograph was taken in Puerto Rico.

"The multitude of palm trees of various kinds, the highest and most beautiful I have ever seen, and an infinite number of other great and green trees; the birds in rich plumage and the lushness of the fields; make this country of such marvelous beauty that it surpasses all others in charms and graces as the day does the night. . ."

The Caribbean region has changed greatly in the 500 years since Columbus's first visit. Most of its superb **rainforests**, which Columbus so beautifully described, were destroyed by later settlers. Those that remain contain a huge variety of wildlife. Clouds of shimmering butterflies feed on the beautiful flowers of tropical plants; multi-colored parrots shriek in the tall trees, while delicate humming-birds take nectar from the flowers growing below. Flocks of pelicans, flamingos, ibis and spoonbills add a splash of color to **lagoons**, and dark buzzards circle in the skies, looking for prey.

In remote rainforest areas of Guyana, Trinidad, Cuba and Belize live shy animals such as wild pigs, small **marsupials** called opossums, and small wildcats like ocelots and margays. Colorful frogs and snakes live in the trees, while many crocodiles lurk in lakes and lagoons. There are also many biting or stinging insects.

Above The scarlet ibis is one of the region's many beautiful birds. Sometimes flocks of them form a red cloud in the sky.

Right In the Zapata Swamps of Cuba live crocodiles like this one.

An underwater paradise

Much of the Caribbean's great wealth of living creatures is found in the warm, tropical waters that surround the islands. Below the surface exists a colorful world of fascinating sea creatures. There are corals of many colors that grow in mysterious shapes. They are a vital source of food for many of the vividly colored tropical fish that inhabit the Caribbean Sea. The water shimmers with shoals of butterfly fish of several species, including the banded, spotfin and foureye. Blue and rainbow parrotfish, which can grow to well over three feet in length, patrol the reefs, gnawing at the coral with their beak-like mouths. Other fish of the region include angelfish and the queen trigger fish.

These fish feeding on the Caribbean coral reef are the rock beauty (left) and the four-eyed butterfly fish (right).

The Caribbean Sea teems with brightly-colored tropical fish. This queen angel fish was photographed near Bermuda.

A female turtle struggles down a Nicaraguan beach having laid her eggs. Few of the young turtles that hatch will survive to reach the sea.

The Caribbean Sea is also known for flying gurnards. These fish cannot actually fly, but are able to leap out of the water and glide for small distances, spreading their large fins in the air as if they were wings. Huge fish such as tuna, which grow to 6 feet (2 m), and blue marlin, which reach 12 feet (4 m), are also found in the region's waters. These, along with the flying fish and some dolphins, are caught by the islands' fishermen. There is one fish that the fishermen try to avoid catching because it is poisonous and very dangerous. It is the great barracuda, a fish almost 6 feet (2 m) in length, that has large jaws and sharp teeth. It is aggressive toward humans and on some occasions has attacked bathers near the shore.

Unlike the barracuda, most sea creatures are harmless to humans. On the contrary, many of them have been harmed by people. Green turtles are one example. Every year the females return to the familiar beaches of some Caribbean islands to lay their eggs. Dragging themselves up the beach at night, they dig out pits in the sand, using their hind flippers. In the pits they lay hundreds of eggs, each about the size of a ping-pong ball. Sad to say, most of the tiny turtles that hatch are caught by their many predators, such as crabs and frigate birds. People are a great enemy and often kill the turtles, sometimes for food. Only a few tiny turtles that manage to escape their enemies and struggle down to the sea stand a chance of survival.

5 Early history

The first Caribbean people were the Ciboney (or Guanahuatebey), the Taino Arawaks and the Caribs, who gave their name to the sea and to the region. The Ciboney were probably the oldest settled people in the region. **Archaeologists** have discovered their sites in Cuba and Haiti. It is most likely that the Ciboney came originally from South America and traveled northward through the string of islands of the Lesser Antilles into the Greater Antilles.

The Arawaks and the Caribs are much better known. When Columbus made Europe's first contact with the region, in 1492, there were probably about three-quarters of a million of them, most of whom lived on Hispaniola, which we now call Haiti and the Dominican Republic. Arawak communities stretched from the Bahamas to the small islands off the coast of Venezuela.

Columbus's contact with the first Caribbean peoples brought disaster. The Ciboney and the Arawaks were mainly killed by European diseases and the actions of Spanish settlers. For just over a hundred years the Spanish controlled the Caribbean as part of its land in the **New World**. By the seventeenth century other European countries began to invade the region,

English Harbor in Antigua is famous for being Lord Nelson's Caribbean base. Today it is used by sailors from all over the world.

Descendants of Arawak peoples still live in parts of Central and South America. This woman and her child live in Guyana.

This grand old house in Havana, Cuba, is built in the Spanish style.

to set up **colonies** for themselves. The Dutch, the French and the English established bases in the region, and settlers began to grow crops like sugar and tobacco. Plantations were hacked out of the lush, wild vegetation. With the local population wiped out, European countries brought in millions of African people as plantation slaves over the next 200 years. The cruel European practice of slavery, and the Africans' resistance to it, dominate the history of the Caribbean.

Large fortunes were made out of sugar plantations in the Caribbean, and wars were fought between European powers to gain control of them. By the start of the nineteenth century, however, much Caribbean land had been exhausted and European-produced beet sugar was beginning to pose a threat to Caribbean cane. As sugar became less profitable, so the need for slaves declined and eventually slavery was abolished.

In place of African slaves Chinese, Indian and Japanese laborers came to work on the plantations, introducing another ingredient to the rich mixture of races which make up the Caribbean today.

6 Recent history

During the twentieth century several major changes occurred in the Caribbean. The building of the Panama Canal, started in the 1880s and completed in 1914, improved the region's trading prospects. The canal was a short cut linking the Pacific and Atlantic oceans. This saved ships from traveling thousands of extra miles around the entire coast of South America.

In 1898 the United States invaded Cuba during the Spanish-American War. Within a few years Cuba was almost a part of the United States. Ever since, the United States has been a major foreign influence in the region.

After the First World War (1914–18), in which many Caribbean people fought, life in the Caribbean region was dominated by poverty and despair. Much needed to be done to improve education, housing, employment, health and social care. In the 1930s the peoples of the Caribbean were forced to act. In most countries of the region there were demonstrations and strikes, which caused tension between workers and police. Great damage was done to property and many people lost their lives. However, out of the unrest came signs of hope – **trade unions**, political parties and leaders who were trusted by the people.

Important dates

1492	European "discovery" of the Caribbean region by Columbus.	1898	United States invades Cuba.
1493–1508	Spanish colonies founded in Hispaniola, Puerto Rico, Jamaica and Cuba.	1914	Panama Canal opens.
		1930s	Period of poverty and unrest.
1517	Spanish bring first African slaves to Caribbean.	1958–62	West Indies **Federation** attempt. United States–Soviet conflict over missiles in Cuba.
1623–32	British establish colonies in St. Kitts, Barbados, St. Croix, Nevis, Antigua and Montserrat.	1962	Jamaica, Trinidad and Tobago become independent.
1634–48	Dutch establish colonies in St. Eustacius, Curaçao, Bonaire and Aruba, and St. Maarten.	1959	Cuban Revolution led by Castro.
		1966	Barbados and Guyana become independent.
1635	French establish colonies in Martinique and Guadeloupe.	1975	Curaçao, Aruba, Bonaire and Suriname become independent.
1650s–1840s	Sugar plantations and African slave trade flourish.	1983	United States invasion of Grenada.
		1988	Hurricane Gilbert.

Two revolutionary men of the Caribbean are pictured here – Maurice Bishop of Grenada (right) and Fidel Castro of Cuba (left). Shortly after this meeting, Maurice Bishop was killed in Grenada.

In 1946 the French islands Martinique, Guadeloupe and Cayenne, or French Guiana, were made *départements* of France with representatives in the **Senate** in Paris. The first islands to gain full **independence** in 1962 were Jamaica and Trinidad. The Dutch islands Curaçao, Aruba, Bonaire and Suriname were granted theirs in 1975.

The Cuban revolution was one of the most dramatic events of the twentieth century. In January 1959 Fidel Castro entered the capital, Havana, having defeated Fulgencio Batista, Cuba's unpopular president. Two years later he announced that Cuba had made a "socialist revolution," firmly linking his country with the USSR. Relations between Cuba and the United States have been tense ever since. In 1961 the United States supported an invasion of Cuba; in 1962 the United States and the USSR were close to war over Soviet missiles in Cuba. This crisis was resolved and Fidel Castro has remained as president, being re-elected in 1988.

To prevent "any more Cubas" in the Caribbean, the United States and Britain kept Guyana from being ruled by a **Marxist** government in the late 1950s and early 1960s. Likewise in the 1970s the United States stepped in to stop Jamaica from becoming too friendly with Cuba. The United States also supported the **Contras** in their war against the Nicaraguan government after the revolution of 1979, and invaded Grenada in 1983.

Who lives in the Caribbean?

There is a strong African influence in the Caribbean. These Jamaicans are playing dominoes, a popular game in the region.

The rich mixture of races who inhabit the Caribbean today is the result of hundreds of years of the region's history. With the exception of the descendents of Caribs, who live on the islands of St. Vincent and Dominica, and **Amerindian** people, who live in Guyana, all those who today live in the Caribbean were transplanted from Europe, Africa and Asia.

A visitor to the region today will find that there is a strong African influence, as well as a Spanish, Dutch, French or British feel to some of the islands. Indian, Chinese and Japanese workers, who came to the region after slavery was abolished, have also contributed to the unique atmosphere of the Caribbean.

The influence of the different Caribbean peoples has spread far beyond the Caribbean region. Descendants of the various Caribbean settlers have emigrated to the United States, Canada and many European countries, bringing their rich culture with them. London, New York, Paris, Amsterdam and Toronto all have large Caribbean communities today. However, due to economic problems in the United States, Canada and Britain, the number of Caribbean immigrants allowed into these countries has been severely restricted.

The mixture of races in the Caribbean has led to some racial **inequality**. In the past most power and wealth were in the hands of whites from Europe and North America. In Barbados and St. Thomas, however, there are whites whose ancestors were never rich or powerful. In countries like Trinidad and Guyana, where the population is made up of a mixture of African and Indian peoples, until recently power lay in the hands of the Africans. Today most people feel that the Caribbean would be much duller without its rich mixture of races.

Right Two Jamaican men wearing Rastafarian dress. This Jamaican movement has spread to many countries.

Below Nicaragua is part of the Caribbean. These people from Masachapa regularly go to meet the fishing boats when they return with their catch.

8 Language and tradition

Languages follow the pattern of colonization of the Caribbean. Cubans, Puerto Ricans, and the people of the Dominican Republic speak Spanish because their countries were Spanish colonies for more than 300 years. Dutch is spoken in Suriname, Curaçao, Bonaire, Saba and St. Maarten, which were once settled by the Dutch. French is the language of Martinique, Guadeloupe, and French Guiana, the French colonies in the Caribbean, as well as of Haiti, a French colony until the beginning of the nineteenth century. English is spoken in Guyana and in Jamaica, Trinidad, Antigua, and all the other islands that make up the British Virgin Islands in the Caribbean. English is also spoken in the United States Virgin Islands, which were bought by the United States from the Danes in 1917.

However, the language picture is not as simple as that. African languages were brought with the slaves to the plantations. Throughout the Caribbean, African languages are spoken, often during religious ceremonies, and are mixed with the dominant language. In Jamaica, English is a second language. The first is "Jamaican dialect" or "Patois," a mixture of English, Spanish, and various African languages.

Posters in Cuba are an important means of communication. They are in Spanish.

French is spoken in Haiti, as shown in the street signs in the market of Port-au-Prince.

The African languages can all be identified. The most dominant one is Twi, which comes from the Akan coast of Ghana, formerly known as the Gold Coast. Many Jamaican people still give African names to their children and the language is rich with African words. Haitian French is completely different from that spoken in Paris, while the Dutch spoken in the region has also been changed over the centuries.

Caribbean tales, folklore and sayings have kept alive African languages as well as African religions and traditions. The Jamaican spider *Anansi* tales come from the African region of Upper Guinea. Anansi is a Jamaican folk hero, cunning and

On St. Kitts in the British Caribbean, a political notice attacks a rival political party. The language is a dialect form of English.

witty, a lovable rascal. Perhaps because he is a great survivor, whatever misfortune strikes him, he appealed especially to African slaves in the Caribbean.

9 | City life

During this century towns and cities in all Caribbean countries have grown. Given the choice, most people would prefer to live in towns and cities. This is because there are more stores, better schools, more jobs, and more things to do and enjoy. In the capital cities, people feel closer to the centers of power where decisions are made.

Many Caribbean capital cities, like San Juan in Puerto Rico, Havana in Cuba, Kingston in Jamaica, Port-au-Prince in Haiti, and Santo Domingo in the Dominican Republic, are ancient Spanish fortified cities. They are also

Over 2 million people live in the Cuban city of Havana. It is the Caribbean's largest capital city.

ports, and are exciting and bustling centers of trade. As a result, all these are famous cities, used to welcoming travelers from all over the world.

There is an excitement and a pace of life in the cities that does not exist elsewhere. Each one has its own particular atmosphere and reputation, sometimes based upon historical events of long ago.

In Cuba the government has tried to deter people from moving into the already overcrowded capital city, Havana. Between 1959 and 1975 it put every effort into making the countryside a more attractive place to live by building new schools, clinics, factories and houses. Meanwhile not even a coat of paint was put on the buildings in Havana. The experiment was not entirely successful but the flow of people from countryside to town, especially to Havana, was slowed down. Managua, the capital city of Nicaragua, filled to overflowing in the 1980s as country people fled there to escape the war going on in their country. Soon the edges of Managua were dotted with shanty towns, which are groups of houses made of any building material that can be found, such as corrugated iron or cardboard.

Above In the port of Bridgetown, Barbados, bananas are being loaded for export.

Below Modern architecture is changing many Caribbean cities. This elegant shopping center is in New Kingston, Jamaica.

10 Home life

Just in one country there can be very different styles of home life. In Cuba, a family living in the countryside in a *bohio* (a traditional simple house made of wood and palm thatch) could well eat better than a middle-class family living in a residential street in Havana. This is because country people grow much of their own food. The home life of a family in a new **provincial** block of flats would be different again. Strangely, the children from all these families could go to the same school. In Haiti there would be an enormous contrast in home life between a well-off, middle-class family in Port-au-Prince, an extremely poor family in a shanty town, and a family in the countryside trying to make a living from growing crops on a patch of soil.

Imagine the contrasts in home life throughout the Caribbean: in the capitals of Nicaragua and Haiti the very poor people live in shanty towns,

Traditional homes, called bohios, are found in the Cuban countryside. They are usually made of wood and have a thatched roof. You can see banana and fig trees growing near this bohio.

Above These flimsy homes, made from waste materials, are in the capital of Nicaragua, Managua, where there are many shanty towns.

and throughout the Caribbean poorer people live in small, flimsy houses in the countryside. At the other end of the scale, very wealthy people live in large, luxurious houses in the capitals of Cuba, Jamaica and Trinidad. Wealthy tourists stay in beautiful hotels, but very few local people, apart from workers, ever see inside them.

The marked contrasts in Caribbean people's living standards can be explained from the region's history. Most Caribbean countries provided agricultural goods, like sugar, cotton and bananas for **export** to Europe and North America. So most people worked on the land. The rich and the better-off tended to live in towns and cities. Inequalities between the towns and the countryside developed, and these still exist today.

This new hotel in Ocho Rios, Jamaica, provides luxury accommodation for wealthy tourists.

11 Shopping and food

Throughout the Caribbean there are colorful, traditional, open-air markets where families shop for most of their daily requirements: fresh fruit (such as pineapples, mangoes, papaya and bananas) and vegetables, freshly caught fish, meat and even some special fiery sauces brought in from the countryside. Country people often travel for hours, sometimes on foot, at other times in buses or on trains, to bring their goods to sell at the market. Women have traditionally taken goods to sell at market, often with children on their backs, as well as sacks of goods on their heads.

In some countries, open-air markets

Colorful, open-air markets supply most Caribbean people with their food, especially fresh fruit and vegetables. This Grenadan market is being held near a supermarket.

exist alongside air-conditioned, American-style supermarkets where frozen food from around the world can be bought, as well as other **imports** such as breakfast cereals and coffee.

Traditional Caribbean cooking is as varied and interesting as the many different peoples who have settled in the region. As one might expect, fish, sometimes preserved in salt, is used in many dishes. Tropical fruit forms a major part of most dishes and is often eaten as a vegetable. The African influence can be seen in the way that **sweet potatoes** and **yams** are cooked in a similar way to rice or potatoes. Breadfruit, green bananas and plantains (a kind of large banana) are also used as vegetables. Indian settlers have introduced many spicy dishes, especially curries. One of the region's specialties is curried goat. On the French islands, chicken and fish are often used in **fricassees**. A popular

dish in many islands is rice and peas cooked in coconut milk.

Rum is naturally a popular Caribbean drink as so much of it is produced there. Because of the hot climate, many people like refreshing drinks such as fresh lemonade, lime juice and the sweet green liquid produced from crushed sugar cane.

Right All kinds of fresh fish are available in Caribbean countries. These fish will make a delicious Haitian-style meal.

Below This Jamaican woman sells coconuts which are often bought as a refreshing drink.

12 Schools and education

Despite improvements in the quality and number of schools and teachers, education is still an enormous problem in most countries of the Caribbean. There are not enough schools and what is taught could be more relevant to the needs of the people living in the Caribbean.

The old powers, Britain, France and the Netherlands, improved the education in their colonies. But their interests were different from those of Caribbean nations today. In the past, the emphasis was on reading, writing and arithmetic. This was just enough education to provide the clerks and **administrators** necessary to run the colonies. More emphasis was put on European writers and European history than Caribbean culture. Even after the colonies became independent, ideas about education have been slow to change. Many school-books still come from Europe and are not aimed at a Caribbean readership. Little education, even at university level, is

In Jamaica private and public schools exist side by side. Here a class meets outdoors.

Left Most secondary school students in Cuba go to "Schools in the Country," where study and practical work are combined.

Below In Cuban schools, pupils are trained in many practical subjects, from electronics to gardening.

linked to Caribbean needs. There are not enough technical or agricultural schools to assist the region's industrial and agricultural development.

Even in recent years education has not been seen as important by many families, especially those living in the countryside. They believe that education is not necessary when there are so few opportunities other than to remain in the same village where they were born. Such attitudes toward education are slowly changing.

Cuba is the exception in the Caribbean. Here, for a long time, education has been seen as the key to the development of the country. A **literacy campaign** was launched in 1961. New schools were built and adults and children were encouraged to continue with their studies. In the mid-1970s Cuba was described as "one huge school" with most of the population, young and old, involved in some kind of study. Cuban economic and social needs were given priority: more doctors and nurses, teachers, scientists, veterinarians, and engineers were trained. Now Cuba provides skilled workers for many **Third World** countries and gives college scholarships to Caribbean students.

13 Sports and recreation

Cricket is played throughout the English-speaking Caribbean. Here a game is played in St. Kitts.

To the great surprise of many, there were Caribbean teams in the 1988 Winter Olympics in the Canadian city of Calgary. The Virgin Islanders and Jamaican competitors were very popular with the spectators but not so successful in their bob-sled events. The fact that people from a region where snow never falls take part in winter sports shows the Caribbean's enthusiasm for sports. Many major league baseball players come from the Caribbean. Caribbean people are great lovers of games of all kinds.

A set of Cuban stamps shows the original Indian peoples playing a game like baseball. That may have been the case but it was the colonial powers who brought their cultures and sports to the Caribbean. As a result baseball, imported by the United States, is the national sport in Cuba, Puerto Rico, the Dominican Republic, Nicaragua and much of Central America. Cricket is played, with great skill and commitment, in the old British Caribbean islands such as Jamaica and Trinidad. The West Indies cricket team has consistently shown its ability to beat the British, who took the game to the islands, just as Cuban baseball teams regularly defeat the American national teams.

Caribbean athletes compete against one another at regional and international events. The region has produced many world-class athletes, like the Quarrie brothers from Jamaica, and Alberto Juantorena from Cuba, who won gold medals in two Olympic Games. The Pan-American Games, like the Olympic Games, give the region the opportunity for its best athletes to compete. The support given to these events by Caribbean governments shows the political importance of sport. This is particularly the case in Cuba. The country has provided talented professional boxers and soccer players. Cuban sportsmen and women regularly win medals in world competitions, especially in athletics, basketball, water polo and boxing.

Right *Runner Alberto Juantorena, twice gold-medallist in the 1976 Montreal Olympics.*

Below *Athletes from throughout the Caribbean compete in the Pan-American Games. Spectators are holding up colored cards to form the coat of arms of Cuba.*

14 Religions and festivals

As a melting pot of cultures, the Caribbean has absorbed many world religions. The Spanish and French brought Roman Catholicism, while the British brought Anglicanism. Africans brought their own religions, which were passed on by word of mouth, to be combined with those brought from Europe. *Pocomania* in Jamaica, *Santeria* in Cuba, and *Vodou* (Voodoo) in Haiti are examples of combined African and European religions. All three religions have large followings. *Santeria* and *Vodou* even exist in the United States which has large Cuban and Haitian communities. Indian, Chinese, Japanese and other migrants to the Caribbean took their religious practices with them. The Indian Hindu and Muslim religions are very strong in Trinidad and Guyana, which have large Indian communities.

Throughout the nineteenth and twentieth centuries, **missionaries** from North America and Europe made the Caribbean an important area of their work. In addition to establishing their own churches, they set up schools and, sometimes, farms, clinics and local projects. The Caribbean Council of Churches, which links the many different churches, has worked to bring economic, social and religious change in the Caribbean.

A traditional Christian baptism is held in a Jamaican river.

Above The Trinidad Carnival is a very exciting event. There is a great variety of costumes.

This bride in Trinidad, Jamaica, is being married according to the same Hindu ceremony that is practiced in India.

Throughout the Caribbean, religion plays an important role. Churches are a thriving part of the community for young and old. Sunday is a day for worship celebrated by many of the people. In Cuba everyone has the right to follow his or her own religion. In the 1980s, attending church has become more popular, especially with the young. This may be a result of Cuba's link with Nicaragua, where members of the government are Catholic priests.

Caribbean festivals and holidays frequently mark religious occasions. The Carnival of the Caribbean, most famous in Trinidad, occurs before Lent. It is an exciting folk festival celebrating Trinidad's history.

15 Culture and the arts

The steel band is a famous and important part of traditional Caribbean music.

The European, African and Asian elements that have come together at different times in the Caribbean's history have fused to make a unique, rich and dynamic culture. Caribbean music, dance, poetry, painting and literature have influenced artists throughout the world.

The Caribbean is probably best known for its music, in which the African element is very strong. Steel bands and **calypso** originated in Trinidad, Jamaica and the other English-speaking Caribbean islands. The **rumba** and the **cha cha** dances began in Cuba, while the **merengue** is most popular in the Dominican Republic. Cuban, Puerto Rican and Jamaican musicians living and working in the United States and Europe have contributed to the development of jazz and salsa music. The Jamaican Bob Marley continues, even after his death, to be popular and to influence reggae music. Rapso and Dub poets, who speak in dialect, also have their fans, even though their work cannot be understood by most people living outside the Caribbean.

Music is just a part of Caribbean culture. The region has produced world-renowned writers and poets, such as Cuba's Nicolas Guillen and Alejo Carpentier; Trinidad's V.S. Naipaul; Guyana's Jan Carew; Aimee Cesaire of Martinique and George

Lamming of Barbados. A new generation of black writers, whose origins lie in the Caribbean, is now well known in North America and Europe.

Caribbean art and sculpture are very varied. The best-known examples are probably the primitive paintings of Haiti, which decorate many churches and cathedrals.

Every five years Carifesta takes place. Held in a different Caribbean country each time, this enjoyable arts festival brings together writers, poets, actors, painters, sculptors, musicians and dancers. The aim is to encourage Caribbean arts in all their forms.

Below The Cuban Escambray Theater involves the audience in the plays, which deal with social and political issues.

These primitive paintings are in the cathedral of Port-au-Prince in Haiti.

16 THE CARIBBEAN
Farming and fishing

The history of the Caribbean is founded on agriculture. The region has an excellent climate and some of the most fertile land in the world. Sugar, tobacco, cotton, spices, citrus fruits and other tropical fruits are exported from the Caribbean to many countries of the world. Cuba is world famous for its tobacco and Havana cigars, although Nicaraguan and Jamaican cigars have become their rivals.

Caribbean people are now realizing their tremendous wealth of agriculture. However, because of the small size of many of the islands and their rugged, mountainous terrain, agricultural land is limited. Curaçao,

for example, consists mainly of rock and has suffered from soil erosion as a result of hot, dry periods followed by heavy rains. Plant pests and diseases can also bring problems – in 1984 Cuba lost a million tons of sugar, and almost all its tobacco crop, due to plant diseases and the bad weather.

In spite of such problems, more people work on the land than in any other occupation in the Caribbean. With unused land still available in countries such as Belize and Guyana, more people could be employed. This would make the region entirely **self-sufficient** in foodstuffs, as well as able to produce more for export.

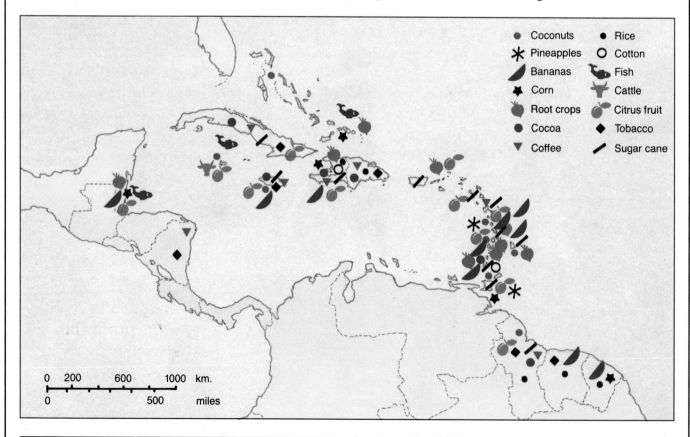

Legend:
- Coconuts
- Pineapples
- Bananas
- Corn
- Root crops
- Cocoa
- Coffee
- Rice
- Cotton
- Fish
- Cattle
- Citrus fruit
- Tobacco
- Sugar cane

0 200 600 1000 km.

0 500 miles

Above Tobacco leaves being harvested in western Cuba, to make Havana cigars.

Above Sugar cane is still cut by hand in some Caribbean countries, although powerful cutting machines are increasingly being used.

Cuba's fishing industry is one of the most efficient in the Caribbean.

The rich diversity of fish that inhabit the Caribbean Sea attracts many fishermen. However, few of them are well paid for their catches and some fishermen struggle to make ends meet.

Cuba has shown what is possible in the fishing industry. Before the revolution, few Cubans ate fish, as it was considered not as good as meat. Cuban tastes, however, have changed and a new, profitable industry has emerged. Since 1959 the Cuban fishing industry has grown large enough to provide enough fish for its own country and a large, profitable export of fish, lobsters and prawns. By contrast, most other Caribbean countries have small fishing fleets but the industry is not yet important.

17 Industry and resources

The Caribbean has vast natural resources: its natural beauty and climate, its fertile soil and a wealth of mineral deposits which have yet to be truly exploited. Bauxite, the raw material for aluminum, is mined in the Dominican Republic, Guyana, Haiti, Jamaica and Suriname. Nickel is Cuba's second most valuable export after sugar, its mining made possible with technology from the USSR. The Dominican Republic, too, is an exporter of nickel from a smelting plant owned by a Canadian company. Cuba and Haiti both possess copper, as well as iron, manganese, chromium and cobalt. The Dominican Republic and Puerto Rico both have large deposits of copper yet to be tapped. Gold is another mineral mined in Guyana and Suriname. Both countries, which have vast areas of almost untouched land, are thought to contain valuable mineral deposits.

Trinidad is the only country in the Caribbean to possess a large amount of petroleum, although Cuba has tiny deposits and high hopes of large off-shore oil wells. But Antigua, Aruba, the Bahamas, Cuba, Curaçao, Puerto Rico, as well as Trinidad and Tobago have refineries. The area is important for American supplies of petroleum. Using profits from oil, the Trinidad

Below The extraction of bauxite, from which aluminum is produced, has proved profitable for several Caribbean countries.

Above Satellite television is becoming popular in many Caribbean countries.

government built a huge and costly steel plant. Unfortunately, no sooner was it built than world demand for steel declined.

In the 1960s most Caribbean countries enjoyed a boom in tourism, largely because Cuba, which had been the most important tourist center, became unpopular due to its revolution. In the 1970s and 1980s, the expected growth of tourism failed to occur, and this created problems for many Caribbean countries. In the 1980s Cuba returned as an important tourist center, attracting Canadian and European tourists who wanted to see for themselves what Cuba and its revolution were like. Cuban tourism differs from the rest of the Caribbean in that hotels and tourist facilities are used by Cubans themselves, and the government has tried to ensure that income from the industry remains in the country.

The superb scenery and climate of St. Lucia provides a wonderful vacation setting for those who can afford it.

18 Transportation

In the past Caribbean countries were encouraged to look to Europe for trade and military and financial support, rather than to make links between themselves. Only recently have they become convinced of some of the advantages of cooperating with one another. As a result, transportation links between Caribbean countries have developed in a haphazard way.

Goods are carried to and from the area by sea. Exports from the Caribbean are mainly carried by foreign shipping. In most of the region's countries there are deep-water ports. Some, like Havana, San

Above *A Tri-Star jet belonging to the Trinidad airline BWIA takes off from Antigua.*

Below *This ferry provides a regular link between the islands of St. Kitts and Nevis.*

CARIBE QUEEN

Below Travelers cling to a heavily-laden Nicaraguan bus.

Juan and Port-of-Spain, are among the world's busiest. People wishing to travel between the islands use sea ferries, like the link between St. Kitts and Nevis.

Four international airlines link the Caribbean with the rest of the world. They are British West Indian Airways (BWIA) from Trinidad, Air Jamaica, Cubana, and Caribbean Airways from Barbados. Leeward Island Air Transport (LIAT) covers all inter-island flights with the exception of Jamaica, Belize and Guyana.

Few Caribbean countries have a good network of railways. Cuba, Guyana and Nicaragua are the exceptions. Buses and communal taxis are the most usual way to travel around. In Haiti people use the *camionettes* and *tap-taps*, which are elaborately painted buses and station wagons. Most bus and taxi systems in the Caribbean have one thing in common – they are nearly always crowded, filled to the brim with passengers, their luggage and sacks of goods, and sometimes live pigs and chickens! When there is no more room inside the buses, goods and furniture are strapped to the outside.

Caribbean people are great travelers. They share a history of traveling over great distances between the islands, such as between Barbados and Cuba, or to Central America and the United States. If inter-island transportation links were improved, more of the people would travel between the islands and discover their great variety.

19 Government

Left In Cuba most adults belong to the People's Militia, which exists to protect the country.

Below Police on Barbados wear uniforms rather like those of the British police. This is because Barbados was once a British colony.

The various systems of government within the Caribbean today are a direct result of the region's history. Some countries are dependent on the countries which once colonized them. Examples are the British Virgin Islands, the Cayman Islands, Montserrat, and the Turks and Caicos Islands. France still possesses three overseas *départements* in the Caribbean, which are Martinique, Guadeloupe and French Guiana.

There are also semidependent countries, which run their own affairs but are dependent upon the former colonial powers for defense. These include the Dutch Antilles, Curaçao, Bonaire, Aruba, St. Eustacius and St. Maarten; and the British Associated States of Antigua, St. Kitts and Nevis, Anguilla, St. Lucia and St. Vincent.

Puerto Rico and the U.S. Virgin Islands are linked to the United States.

Some Caribbean states have become totally independent of their former colonial powers. They are Belize, Jamaica, Barbados, Haiti, Cuba, Dominica, the Bahamas, Grenada, the Dominican Republic, Guyana, Suriname, and Trinidad and Tobago.

Most of the former British Caribbean countries have chosen to remain within the **Commonwealth** with the British monarch as Head of State. Guyana, however, declared itself an independent **republic** in 1966. Puerto Rico has tried to change its status as a commonwealth of the United States, but America has repeatedly blocked these attempts.

The system of government in the "British" Caribbean is similar to the British system itself. There are two houses of parliament, one elected, the other appointed. Puerto Rico's system of an elected Governor, Senate and House of Representatives is taken directly from the United States. Revolutionary Cuba introduced a new system of government in 1976. It is called *People's Power*, and has made the country easier to govern because it has been divided up into smaller provinces and elected assemblies. Independent Haiti, the poorest country in the Caribbean, is trying to make a new, free system of government after the unpopular Duvaliers fled the country in 1986, having run Haiti as a **dictatorship** for nearly thirty years.

The grand residence of the Jamaican Prime Minister in Kingston.

20 The future for wildlife

The Caribbean faces a number of problems as it looks to the future. Many of them concern the landscape of the region. As we have already seen, agriculture is vital to the Caribbean and provides a large part of its income. In recent times there has been a fall in the price of tropical goods, like sugar, which the region exports all over the world. This is partly due to the European Economic Community's policy of giving money to European beet sugar production. The world economic crisis has also lowered all agricultural and mineral prices. However, the Caribbean must pay very high prices to buy machinery from other countries. So the region needs to sell more sugar or bauxite, to be able to pay for such goods.

If the Caribbean economy is to be more successful in future, the region will have to continue to develop its natural resources. However, large-scale mining of mineral deposits, increased agricultural production and the development of tourism will all require more of the region's land. Already much of the natural vegetation has been cleared from

This beautiful forest, and the animals that live in it, are protected for the future. It is the Caribbean National Forest in Puerto Rico.

Left The margay, a small wild cat that lives in remote rainforest areas of the Caribbean, is now an endangered species.

The Jabiru, or black-necked stork, has a wing span of up to 3.5 m (10.5 ft). A large colony of these birds are protected in Crooked Tree Wildlife Sanctuary in Belize.

many of the islands. Belize still contains a large area of unspoiled rainforest that is rich in wildlife, but the country is under pressure to make more money from its natural resources. This would mean clearing much of the rainforest to create agricultural land. As rainforests are cleared, the animals that live in them are made homeless and soon die.

One way to preserve wildlife is to create nature reserves. The Caribbean National Forest is an area of protected rainforest in Puerto Rico. It was created when people realized that only 3 percent of Puerto Rican natural forest was left untouched. Now it is a safe haven for thousands of plants and animals, as well as a tourist attraction. In the mid 1980s several wildlife sanctuaries were created on Belize, to preserve some of the country's unique wildlife.

As Caribbean countries plan how to develop their resources in the future, it is hoped that they will make greater efforts to preserve the wildlife and natural beauty of the region.

21 The future of the people

In the future one of the main challenges facing the Caribbean will be how the region relates to other countries of the world. The revolutions that have taken place in some Caribbean countries have had a dramatic effect on other countries in the region. They have also affected the region's relationships with the superpowers – the United States and the USSR. Cuba, Nicaragua, Guyana, Grenada and Jamaica have all tried a revolutionary alternative to the traditional system of government in the Caribbean. This has led to considerable conflict with the United States, which is concerned that the region should not be closely linked with the USSR. The United States has intervened on many occasions to

A Soviet warship and submarine on a friendly visit to Cuba. The close relationship of these two countries has caused concern to the U.S.

ensure that there is no repetition of the Cuban revolution.

Throughout this century, the United States has increased its influence in the Caribbean. In fact, the Caribbean has been described as "America's backyard." If that is so, then the yard has grown to stretch from Florida to Cuba, Nicaragua and Grenada, over 600 km (370 mi) away. Some Caribbean countries see their future closely linked with the United States. Jamaica, Antigua and Dominica have all supported the United States on issues like the invasion of Grenada, and expect the United States to support them in return.

Another challenge to the Caribbean is how all the countries within the region relate to one another. As we have seen, the Caribbean consists of many very different countries. Naturally, each country wishes to promote its best interests. Despite some attempts at cooperation between the countries of the Caribbean, such as CARICOM (the Caribbean Common Market), there is no urgency about uniting all the countries of the region.

The people of the Caribbean have great courage, resourcefulness and commitment. Once they can act together and help one another, and can responsibly harness their region's wealth of natural resources, then they can expect a brighter future.

Above The elaborate costume of this man at the Trinidad Carnival shows that slavery has not been forgotten, although it was abolished in the Caribbean long ago.

Below The national flags of some of the many Caribbean countries. The future strength of the region depends on how closely the different countries can act together.

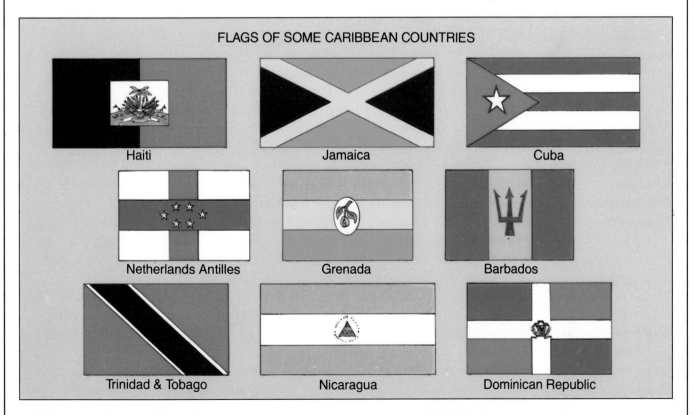

FLAGS OF SOME CARIBBEAN COUNTRIES

Haiti

Jamaica

Cuba

Netherlands Antilles

Grenada

Barbados

Trinidad & Tobago

Nicaragua

Dominican Republic

Glossary

Administrators The people who run the government or a business.

Amerindian The name of the original peoples of the Americas. The word comes from "American Indian."

Archaeologist A person who studies how people lived in the past by digging up the remains of buried cities.

Calypso A popular, amusing Caribbean song accompanied by a strong beat.

Cha cha A ballroom dance using small steps and swaying hip movements.

Colony A country that belongs to, and is ruled by, another country.

Commonwealth A group of countries that now have their own governments but were once ruled by Britain.

Contras A group of people in Nicaragua who are acting against the government. The Spanish word *contra* means "against" or being opposed to.

Culture The customs, beliefs and artistic skills of a group of people of a particular country.

Dictatorship The ruling of a country by a group of people who have total power over the inhabitants of that country.

Exploit To use to the full the resources provided by nature; for example, minerals.

Export A product that one country sells to another.

Federation A group of countries that unite to become stronger and to help one another.

Fertile (of soil) Very rich and nourishing, encouraging the growth of plants.

Fricassee A stew of meat in a white sauce.

Import A product that one country buys from another.

Independence Being totally separate from any other country.

Inequality Treating some people less fairly than others.

Lagoon A pond of shallow water, usually separated from the sea by low banks of sand.

Literacy campaign An effort by a government to ensure that more people will learn how to read. Literacy is the ability to read.

Marsupials Animals with pouches in which their young develop; for example, kangaroos.

Marxism A political theory put forward by Karl Marx and Friedrich Engels. It is the basis of Communism, the political system of the USSR and many Eastern European countries.

Merengue A rhythmical Caribbean dance.

Missionary A person sent out for religious purposes, often to distant countries.

New World The western part of the world, especially the Americas.

Provincial A word used to describe the areas outside the capital or main cities of a country.

Rainforest A lush, moist forest found in parts of the world between the tropics of Capricorn and Cancer, where the temperature is warm and there is regular rainfall throughout the year.

Republic A country that is ruled by a president of its choice, not by a king or queen.

Rumba A Cuban dance with a strong beat.

Self-sufficient Able to produce all the food one needs.

Senate One of the two French houses of parliament.

Sweet potato A vegetable grown in the Caribbean region; it has a fleshy root.

Third World The countries of Africa, Asia and Latin America.

Trade union An organization of workers who join together to improve the working conditions and payment provided by their employer.

Yam A type of sweet potato.

Books to read

Carroll, Raymond. *The Caribbean: The Issues in U.S. Relations* (Franklin Watts, 1984)

Dolan, Edward J., and Scariano, Margaret M. *Cuba and the United States: Troubled Neighbors* (Franklin Watts, 1987)

Gelman, Rita Golden. *Inside Nicaragua: Young People's Dreams and Fears* (Franklin Watts, 1988)

Griffiths, John. *We Live in the Caribbean* (Bookwright Press, 1985)

Hanmer, Trudy J. *Haiti* (Franklin Watts, 1987)

Hanmer, Trudy J. *Nicaragua* (Franklin Watts, 1986)

Lye, Keith. *Take a Trip to Cuba* (Franklin Watts, 1987)

Lye, Keith. *Take a Trip to Jamaica* (Franklin Watts, 1988)

Paraiso, Aviva. *Caribbean Food and Drink* (Bookwright Press, 1989)

Picture acknowledgments

The photographs in this book were taken by the following: Chapel Studios 31 (above), 45; Bruce Coleman Limited *cover* (Giorgio Gualco), 7 (below) and 10 (Jane Burton), 9 (above/Henry Ausloos), 43 (above/L C Marigo), (below/V Serventy); John Griffiths 8, 11 (right), 12, 15, 17 (below), 19 (below), 23 (above), 27, 28, 29, 31 (below), 33, 35, 38, 39 (below), 40 (below), 41, 42 and 44; Hutchison Library 5 and 24 (Sarah Errington), 21 (above/Tony Hardwell); Tony Morrison 13 (left); Oxford Scientific Films 11 (left/Zig Leszczynski); Topham Picture Library 32; John Wright 9 (below), 13 (right), 16, 17 (above), 18, 19 (top), 20, 21 (below), 22, 23 (below), 25, 26, 30, 36, 39, 40; ZEFA *frontispiece* and 6 (K Kerth), 7 (top/Berssenbru) 37.

Index